The SLUG and the PUG

Short Vowel Sounds with Consonant Blends

Brian P. Cleary

Illustrations by Jason Miskimins

Consultant:
Alice M. Maday
PhD in Early Childhood Education with a Focus in Literacy
Assistant Professor, Retired
Department of Curriculum and Instruction
University of Minnesota

Lerner Publications ◆ Minneapolis

To Juniper

Text copyright © 2022 by Brian P. Cleary
Illustrations copyright © 2022 by Lerner Publishing Group, Inc.

Lerner Publications Company
An imprint of Lerner Publishing Group, Inc.
241 First Avenue North
Minneapolis, MN 55401 USA

For reading levels and more information, look up this title at www.lernerbooks.com.

Main body text set in Mikado.
Typeface provided by HVD.

Library of Congress Cataloging-in-Publication Data

Names: Cleary, Brian P., 1959– author. | Miskimins, Jason, illustrator. | Maday, Alice M., consultant.
Title: The slug and the pug : short vowel sounds with consonant blends / Brian P. Cleary ; illustrations by Jason Miskimins ; consultant, Alice M. Maday.
Description: Minneapolis : Lerner Publications, [2022] | Series: Phonics fun | Audience: Ages 4–8 | Audience: Grades 2–3 | Summary: "The plum on the drum is glum. With rhyming, carefully leveled text and comedic, colorful illustrations, this book provides plenty of examples of short vowel sounds with consonant blends and encourages readers to try the sounds for themselves"– Provided by publisher.
Identifiers: LCCN 2021022685 (print) | LCCN 2021022686 (ebook) | ISBN 9781728440866 (library binding) | ISBN 9781728448497 (paperback) | ISBN 9781728444901 (ebook)
Subjects: LCSH: English language—Vowels—Juvenile literature. | English language—Consonants—Juvenile literature. | English language—Phonetics—Juvenile literature.
Classification: LCC PE1157 .C558 2022 (print) | LCC PE1157 (ebook) | DDC 428.1/3—dc23

LC record available at https://lccn.loc.gov/2021022685
LC ebook record available at https://lccn.loc.gov/2021022686

Manufactured in the United States of America
1-49856-49703-9/2/2021

Dear Parents and Educators,

As a former adult literacy coach and the father of three children, I know that learning to read isn't always easy. That's why I developed **Phonics Fun**—a series that employs a combination of devices to help children learn to read. This book uses rhyme, repetition, illustration, and phonics to introduce young readers to short vowel sounds with consonant blends. Words in bold all feature short vowel sounds with consonant blends.

The bridge to literacy is one of the most important we will ever cross. It's my hope that the Phonics Fun series will help new readers to hop, gallop, and skip from one side to the other!

Sincerely,

Brian P. Cleary

Note to Readers

This book is all about short vowel sounds with consonant blends. You can hear short vowel sounds and consonant blends in words like **clam** and **sled**. The **bold** words in this book have short vowel sounds with consonant blends. They also rhyme!

The **plum** on the **drum** is **glum**.

The **clam swam** in the **tram.**

tram

6

The **drink** from the **rink** had such a **stink**, it made him **blink**.

Fred sped his **sled** by the bed.

slop

Stop, drop, and **flop** in the **slop.**

grass

glass

brass

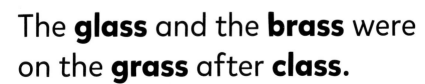

The **glass** and the **brass** were on the **grass** after **class**.

The **grid slid** and made the kid **skid.**

skid

Scott got to **trot** with **Spot** to the **plot.**

snug

The **slug** and pug slept **snug** on the rug by the **plug.**

Make Your Own

Use the words on these pages to write a story with short vowel sounds and consonant blends!

plum

snug

stop

grump

frog

brim

slug

drum

stump

drop

skim

clog

Poet, literacy enthusiast, and word nerd **Brian P. Cleary** "grew up" in one of the largest creative divisions in the world, where he has put words in the mouths of Dolly Parton, William Shatner, and Kevin Nealon. He has written many best-selling grammar and poetry books for young readers.

Jason Miskimins graduated from the Columbus College of Art & Design in 2003. He works as an illustrator of books and greeting cards.

Alice M. Maday has a master's degree in early childhood education from Butler University and a PhD in early childhood education, with a focus on literacy, from the University of Minnesota. Her research interests include kindergarten curriculum, emergent literacy, parent and teacher expectations, and the place of preschool in the reading readiness process.